Accidental Genius

Science Puzzles for Clever Kids

ELEPHANTS, TIGERS, GORILLAS, and SLOTHS

Rain Forest and Jungle Biomes

Alix Wood

WINDMILL BOOKS

Published in 2024 by Windmill Books,
an Imprint of Rosen Publishing
2544 Clinton Street
Buffalo, NY 14224

Written, designed and illustrated by Alix Wood
All other images © AdobeStock Images

Cataloging-in-Publication Data

Names: Wood, Alix.
Title: Elephants, tigers, gorillas, and sloths: rain forest and jungle biomes / Alix Wood.
Description: Buffalo, New York : Windmill Books, 2024. | Series: Accidental genius | Includes glossary and index.
Identifiers: ISBN 9781538394878 (pbk.) | ISBN 9781538394885 (library bound) | ISBN 9781538394892 (ebook)
Subjects: LCSH: Rain forest ecology--Juvenile literature. | Jungle ecology--Juvenile literature. | Games--Juvenile literature. | Picture puzzles--Juvenile literature.
Classification: LCC QH541.5.R27 W66 2024 | DDC 577.34--dc23

Printed in the United States of America

CPSIA Compliance Information: Batch CSWM24
For Further Information contact Rosen Publishing at 1-800-237-9932

Find us on

Contents

What Is a Rain Forest?

A rain forest is a forest with tall trees and warm, wet weather. The rain forest is home to hundreds of amazing animals.

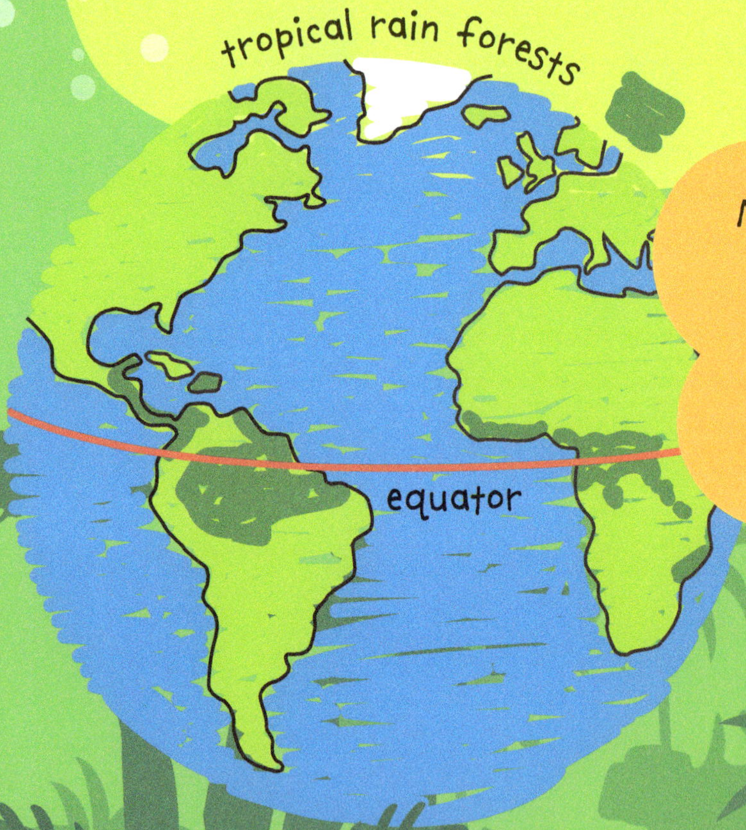

Most rain forests are in hot, wet tropical areas near the equator. The equator is an imaginary line around the center of the Earth.

Rain forests can get over 1 inch (2.5 cm) of rain almost every day of the year!

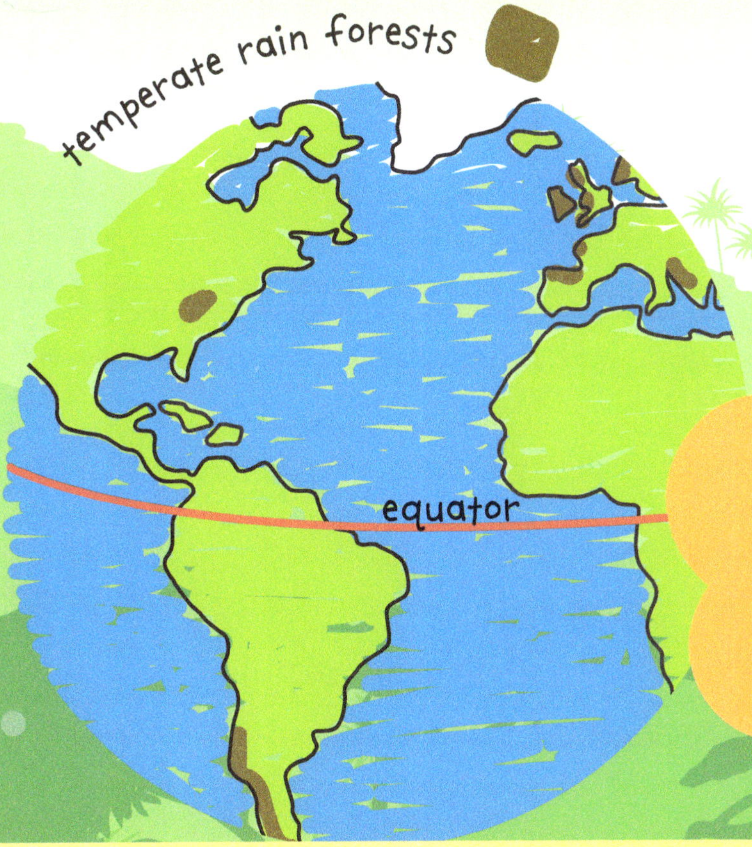

Temperate rain forests are in cooler areas, near the coast. Temperate means not too hot and not too cold.

Word Search

Find 8 animals that might live in a tropical rain forest. Copy, print, or trace the puzzle if you're sharing this book.

B	U	T	T	E	R	F	L	Y	E
E	F	I	N	S	G	B	U	L	N
L	S	G	O	R	I	L	L	A	R
E	V	E	W	T	N	E	T	S	E
P	S	R	T	A	W	U	G	P	S
H	D	V	C	M	G	I	H	R	H
A	C	U	A	N	S	T	N	L	T
N	O	I	A	L	P	N	K	G	O
T	S	R	M	A	C	A	W	I	L
U	O	Q	U	T	V	S	E	R	S

TIGER
TOUCAN
SLOTH
GORILLA
ELEPHANT
MACAW
ORANGUTAN
BUTTERFLY

What Is a Jungle?

A jungle is an area covered in low, tangled plants. Thick jungle usually grows along rivers. Away from the river, the trees get taller. They keep out the sunlight, so not much can grow close to the ground.

Who is hiding in the jungle?

Jungle tigers hunt by creeping up on their prey. Their stripes help hide them. Stripes of sunlight shine between the plant stems. The stems and leaves look stripy, too.

If tigers need to hide in green jungle, why are they orange? Because their favorite meal of deer or boar are color-blind! They can't tell the difference between red and green. So, to them, orange tigers match the jungle very well.

Color It In

Copy, print, or trace the picture if you are sharing this book with others.

Life in a Rain Forest

Many animals make their homes in the warm, damp rain forest. The plants and trees give food and shelter. Some animals rely on each other for their food, too.

Plants

Bromeliad plants grow on trees. They catch rainwater in their leaves. Small frogs live and breed in the puddles!

Insects

Leaf-cutter ants cut up leaves and take them to their nests. They let the leaves rot to grow fungus, which they eat.

Birds

Macaws eat seeds, nuts, fruits, berries, and leaf buds. Their strong beak is perfect for breaking nuts open.

Big Cats

Jaguars are fierce hunters. They hunt deer, iguanas, armadillos, fish, birds, and monkeys.

Every year, scientists discover new animals and plants in the rain forest that no one has seen before!

Monkeys

Squirrel monkeys eat fruit and insects. They also eat plants, nuts, seeds, eggs, small birds, and bats.

A food chain is a sequence showing who eats who. On a separate sheet of paper, put this food chain in the right order.

1 ? eats 2 ? eats 3 ?

a) squirrel monkey

b) jaguar

c) plants

Make a Rain Forest in a Jar

You will need: a jar with lid, soil, pebbles and stones, small plants and moss

1. Fill the jar with layers of pebbles and soil.
2. Add small plants, moss, and stones.
3. Water your rain forest. Put on the lid and place the jar in daylight, but not direct sunlight.
4. Open the jar for a while every few days to keep it from getting moldy.

The warmth of the daylight turns the water in the jar into vapor. The vapor condenses on the cool glass and falls back down as rain. The jar acts a little like the rain forest trees, trapping the dampness.

Layers of Forest

Most rain forests have four layers. Each layer gets a different amount of sunshine and rain. Because of this, certain animals and plants prefer to live in different layers.

EMERGENT LAYER
The top layer of a rain forest has trees as tall as skyscrapers! It is sunny and windy.

THE CANOPY
Most trees grow to this height. Their leaves form an umbrella over the forest below.

THE UNDERSTORY
Vines and small trees grow in the warm, dappled shade of the understory.

FOREST FLOOR
Hardly any sunlight reaches the forest floor. It is dark and damp.

Match the Animal to the Forest Layer

Use tracing paper or write your answers on a separate sheet of paper.

EMERGENT LAYER
I live in the treetops.
I glide from tree to tree.

sloth

anteater

CANOPY
I hang upside down from branches in the canopy.

THE UNDERSTORY
My spotted fur helps me hide in dappled shade.

sugar glider

jaguar

FOREST FLOOR
I snuffle along the ground looking for ants to eat.

Explore Dappled Shade

On a sunny day, find a leafy tree. Place a large sheet of paper on the ground where its shadow falls. Using a pencil, trace around the shadow shapes of the twigs and leaves. Can you see how a jaguar might be hidden by those shadow shapes?

Life at the Top

It's a long way up to the top layer of the rain forest. Most rain forest animals that live there can either fly or glide. Flying insects, bats, birds, and sugar gliders call the treetops their home. Small monkeys climb up there, too.

Find 10 butterflies in this picture.

Now You See Me! Now You Don't!

Pilots flying over the Amazon rain forest sometimes see bright blue morpho butterflies flying above the trees! Their wings can be up to eight inches (20.3 cm) wide. The backs of their wings are brown. As they flap their wings shut, they almost disappear against the trees.

Design your own colorful butterfly.

Color It In

Copy, print, or trace the picture if you are sharing this book with others.

The Canopy

Most rain forest plants and animals live in the rain forest canopy. The thick canopy shelters them from rain. It also traps damp air and blocks out sunlight. Many animals find all the food and shelter they need there. They may never go to the forest floor.

Make a Rain Forest Canopy

You will need: some cardboard tubes, green tissue paper or thin card stock, tape, markers, a small box, some rice, a flashlight

1. Color the tubes to look like tree trunks using brown and black markers.

2. Cut the green paper into leaf shapes. Tape one end of each leaf inside the top of the tubes. Put five or six leaves on each tree.

3. Put your trees in the box.

4. Sprinkle rice over the trees. The rice acts like rain. Shine the flashlight onto the canopy. Did much rice or light reach the forest floor?

Why not decorate your rain forest with toy animals and put leaves on the forest floor?

Sloths sleep up to 20 hours a day in the canopy. They move so slowly that small plants grow on their fur!

Many types of monkeys swing through the trees of the canopy.

Most rain forest birds live in the canopy. There are parrots, macaws, toucans, and hummingbirds.

Orangutans make themselves a new nest in the canopy every single night.

Lemurs eat fruit and flowers. They help create new plants by spreading pollen and seeds that get stuck on their fur!

Understory Life

Plants here need large leaves to get enough energy from the tiny specks of sunlight. Insects love the warm, damp shelter of the understory. Snakes, frogs, birds, and bats make their home here.

The bright colors of tiny poison dart frogs warn predators not to eat them. They ooze deadly poison from their skin!

The fire-bellied snake eats frogs. It is the only snake that can eat poison dart frogs.

Can you see what the frog might eat?

A rain forest canopy is so thick, it can take 10 minutes for a raindrop to fall through it to the rain forest floor!

Raindrop Maze

Using your finger, complete the maze to find out which raindrop will find its way to the forest floor.

The Forest Floor

The rain forest floor is dark, hot, and damp. Fallen leaves and branches cover the ground. Insects make their home in the forest litter. The forest floor is also home to large mammals. You might find tigers in an Asian rain forest. Gorillas and elephants live in African rain forests. Capybara and anteaters roam the forest floors of South America.

Rain Forest Layer Sudoku

Each red square, row, and column must have an animal from each rain forest layer. Can you find the missing ones? Write your answers on a separate sheet of paper.

1.  emergent layer
2.  canopy
3.  understory
4.  forest floor

Match the name to the animal

1. 

2. 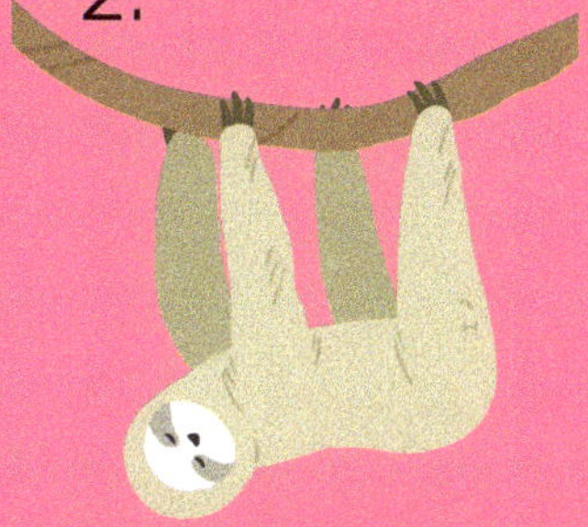

3. 

4. 

- capybara
- sugar glider
- poison dart frog
- sloth

Look Out! Elephants

Can you imagine a huge African elephant crashing through the rain forest? Their huge, curved tusks might get caught in the vines! Their size and pale color would make it difficult for them to hide, too. However, African forest elephants have adapted to live in their dense, dark surroundings.

Helpful Elephants!

Forest elephants may eat or trample plants, bark, fruit, and roots. However, they are really good for the rain forest, too. For instance, the pathways they clear help other animals travel around.

When forest elephants eat fruit, the seeds eventually come out in their poop. This helps move seeds to new areas. The seeds grow really well in their poop, too!

Copy, print, or trace the picture if you are sharing this book with others.

Connect the Dots

Who is rushing to see the big forest elephant?

Color It In

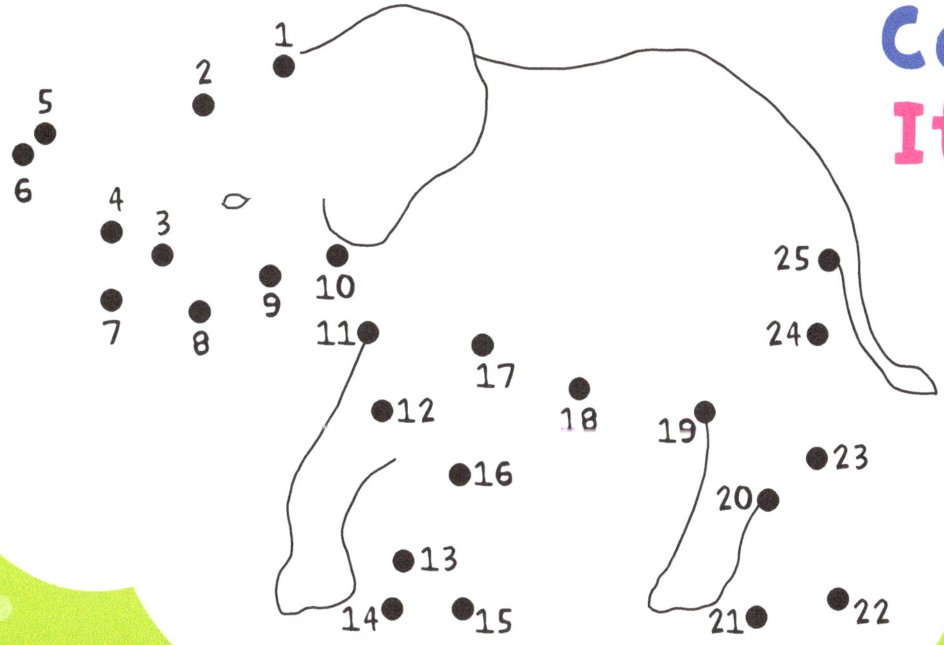

Slow Sloths

Sloths are the slowest-moving mammals on Earth. They can't run from predators who want to eat them. Green plants and brown beetles living on their fur help them blend into the trees. However, once a week, they have to risk climbing out of the trees to go to the bathroom.

jaguar

A sloth's main predators are jaguars, ocelots, and harpy eagles. These predators use their sense of sight to hunt. Sloths move incredibly slowly so that these sharp-eyed predators don't notice them move!

ocelot

harpy eagle

Be as Slow as a Sloth: Play Sly Fox

You will need: some friends, a wall, a large open space

One player (the fox) faces the wall. The fox counts to five while the other players slowly sneak up on them. At the count of five, the fox turns around. If the fox spots a player moving, that player must go back to the start. Whoever touches the fox's back first is the winner.

Slow and Safe

Using your finger, help the sloth reach the forest floor. It can't go on any vines or branches with predators on them.

Big-Beaked Toucans

Toucans have a long, sharp, colorful beak. They use their beak to reach fruit high up in the trees. A toucan's beak is one-third of the bird's total length!

Why do birds have different-shaped beaks? Scientist Charles Darwin found that birds' beaks adapt over time to be perfect for the food they eat. Pointy beaks are great for picking seeds out of rocks. Wide beaks are best for scooping.

Find the Best Beak for the Job

You will need: some candy, a drinking straw, two paper cups, some rocks, a timer

1. Fold the straw in half to make a pointy beak. Flatten one paper cup to make a wide beak.
2. Scatter some food on a table. Set a timer for one minute. Try each beak and see how many candies you can get into the other paper cup in that time.
3. Scatter rocks among the candy. Set the timer. Spit out any rocks you get. Which beak worked best?

Color It In

Copy, print, or trace the picture if you are sharing this book with others.

Rain Forest Monkeys

Monkeys are great climbers and spend most of their days in the trees. Like us, monkeys have thumbs that can grip. This means they can climb well and use tools. Many types of monkey from North, South, and Central America can even grip things using their tails!

Spider monkeys spend most of their time in the canopy finding fruits, plants, and seeds to eat. They get their name from their long, spidery legs and tail.

You hear howler monkeys before you see them. Their call can be heard up to 3 miles (4.8 km) away! Howler monkeys are large, with a tail five times as long as their body!

Marmoset monkeys are very small. They can climb the tallest trees to hunt for insects.

Tamarin monkey mothers usually have twins. Emperor tamarins have mustaches!

How can you tell apes and monkeys apart? Look for a tail. Apes (chimpanzees, gorillas, orangutans, and gibbons) do not have tails. Almost all monkeys do have tails.

Ape or Monkey?

Can you spot which of these are monkeys?

baboon

chimpanzee

golden tamarin

orangutan

Mountain Gorillas

Gorillas are big apes. They live in the rain forests of Africa in family groups known as "troops." Male mountain gorillas are the same height as a human man, and weigh about twice as much! Adult male mountain gorillas are called silverbacks because of a silver patch of hair on their backs.

Silverbacks fiercely protect their troop from invaders. They hit their chest with their fists, throw plants, stamp their feet, and slap the ground. They charge on all fours, too!

Gorillas are actually gentle, shy animals. The troop spends its day moving from place to place looking for plants to eat. Every evening, the gorillas build new nests in the trees or grass to sleep in.

Spot the Difference

Can you find 7 differences between these two pictures of a gorilla troop?

River Life

Lots of rainfall means tropical rain forests have some of the largest rivers in the world! The huge Amazon river snakes through the Amazon rain forest. It is home to all kinds of wildlife. Enormous alligator-like black caiman lurk in the water. They grab capybaras or deer as they come to the river to drink. They also eat scary piranha fish.

Black caimans are reptiles. Reptiles lay eggs. Can you find 8 caiman eggs by the water's edge?

Piranhas

Piranha fish may be small, but they are fierce. They hunt their prey in groups. Connect the dots to see why piranhas are so scary.

Copy, print, or trace the puzzle if you are sharing this book with others.

Do dolphins really live in the rain forest? Amazingly, yes! The Amazon River is home to pink river dolphins.

Clever Plants

Plants need water, nutrients, air, space, and sunlight to grow. Some plants have developed very clever ways to survive in the crowded, dark rain forest!

Vines climb up the tree trunks to reach the sunlight.

Too much rain can rot plants. Many rain forest plants' leaves have curved tips so the rain runs off.

Poor soil means the trees have shallow underground roots. Tall trees grow buttress roots high up their trunks, which give them more support.

Forest floor plants have large leaves to collect as much sunlight as they can.

Can you find three hummingbirds like this one?

How Do Buttress Roots Work?

You will need: two pencils, modeling clay

Make a flat circle of modeling clay. Push one end of a pencil into the circle. Make a cone of modeling clay. Push the second pencil into the top of the cone. Which pencil is the least wobbly?

Strangler fig seeds start to grow in the canopy. Their roots grow down a tree trunk toward the soil. Eventually, strangler fig roots strangle that tree!

Bromeliads' waxy leaves form a bowl that catches rain. Instead of needing roots to get water, they drink through their leaves.

Pitcher plants eat meat! They make a sweet liquid that attracts insects and small mammals. Their prey falls into their tall cups. The cup walls are slippery so they cannot escape.

Rain Forest Frogs

Frogs are amphibians. Amphibians live the first part of their lives in water. As adults, they live on land. Many frogs live in rain forests and jungle. Brightly colored frogs are usually poisonous. Their color warns predators not to eat them. Other frogs use camouflage to hide from predators. Some do a little of both!

camouflage

In daytime, red-eyed tree frogs sleep clinging to the underside of leaves. With their eyes closed and their legs tucked in, only their green parts show. They are perfectly hidden.

startle coloration

When threatened, they open their red eyes and flash their orange feet and bright sides. This startles predators, giving the frog time to hop to safety!

Frogs' feet ooze wet slime. This helps the suction pads on their toes cling to surfaces!

Female poison dart frogs lay their eggs on the forest floor. When the eggs hatch, the parents carry the tadpoles on their backs to a puddle, often in the center of a bromeliad plant! The mother then lays more eggs for the tadpoles to eat.

Is this a tree frog or a poison dart frog? Color this picture to find out.

Use these colors

1
2
3
4
5

Copy, print, or trace the picture if you are sharing this book with others.

Cold-Blooded Snakes

The tropical rain forest is a perfect place for snakes. Snakes are reptiles. Reptiles are cold-blooded. That means their body temperature changes with the temperature around them. A warm rain forest means they will always be warm and comfortable.

Rain Forest Snakes

Amazing Snake Facts

1. They don't have eyelids.
2. They swallow their food whole.
3. Their flexible jaws let them eat prey bigger than their head.
4. They are covered in scales
5. They smell using their tongue.

Make a Paper Chain Snake

You will need: colored paper, scissors, ruler, pencil, markers, glue stick or tape

1. Place two sheets of colored paper on top of each other. Fold both in half lengthwise.
2. Draw ruler-wide strips across the top sheet of paper. You should get 8 or 9 strips.
3. Cut along the fold. Then cut along the strips.
4. Make one strip into a circle. Glue or tape the overlap in place. Thread a second strip through the circle. Make it into a circle and glue or tape in place. Repeat until you have a long snake.

5. Mark out two slightly longer ruler-wide strips. Taper the end of one strip into a tail. Draw a head shape on the end of the other strip. Cut them out. Thread them onto each end of your snake. Glue or tape them in place.

6. Cut out a red forked tongue and glue it on. Now decorate your snake using markers.

Most rain forest snakes are green or brown. Why do you think that is?

Rain Forest Big Cat

Jaguars hunt in South America's rain forests. They are the third-largest cat in the world. Their fur is usually light orange-brown with black spots. A few jaguars have dark fur, so you can hardly see their spots. Jaguars are fearsome hunters.

Jaguars sometimes climb trees to surprise their prey from above. They kill their prey with a powerful bite.

Tapirs use their long snout to grab leaves and fruit. They are a favorite food of the jaguar!

Jaguars are good swimmers. In the water, they can catch fish, turtles, or caimans.

Shadow Match

What animals are being hunted by the jaguar?

1.

2.

3.

4.

monkey

tapir

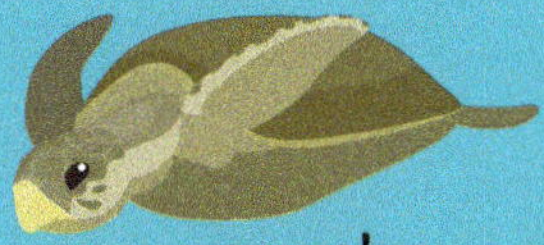

turtle

anteater

Word Search

Can you find 8 animals that need to watch out if a jaguar is about? Copy, print, or trace the puzzle if you're sharing this book.

B	E	F	A	L	M	O	Z	L	D
L	C	A	I	M	A	N	S	E	U
I	A	H	R	S	C	X	E	Y	R
K	P	E	K	T	H	R	E	M	S
W	Y	O	T	N	T	K	I	E	E
O	B	C	R	G	N	I	D	L	L
S	A	S	L	O	T	H	S	R	T
V	R	O	M	L	E	N	K	P	R
B	A	P	I	N	R	S	H	C	U
U	S	L	M	B	I	R	D	S	T

FISH
TURTLES
CAIMANS
DEER
CAPYBARAS
BIRDS
MONKEYS
SLOTHS

Giant Bird Eater!

Spiders and insects are usually food for birds. However, a certain rain forest creepy-crawly is so big it gets its revenge. It can eat birds—and just about anything smaller than it is!

Copy, print, or trace the picture if you are sharing this book.

Connect the Dots

What could this bird eater be? Connect the dots to find out.

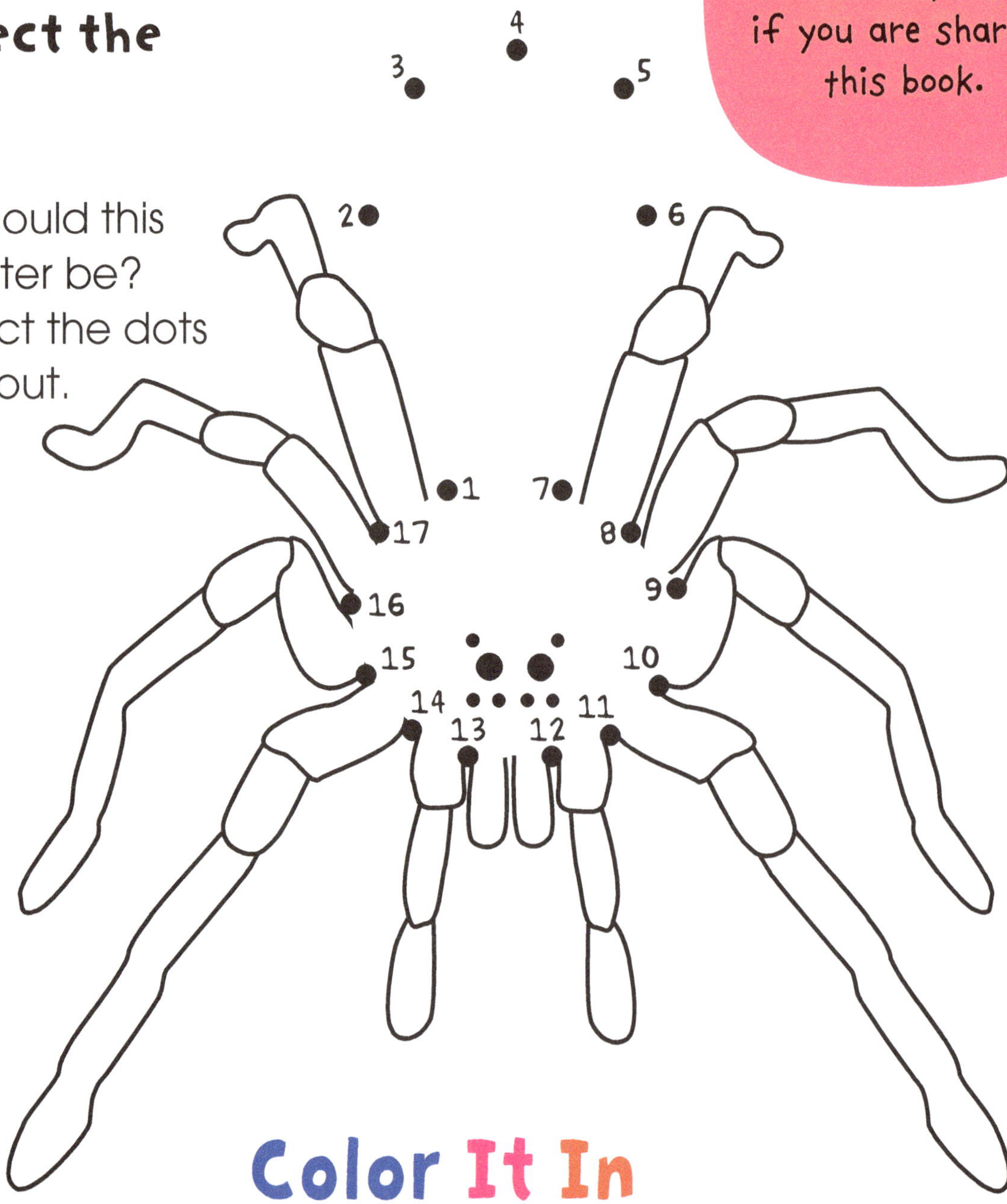

Color It In

Goliath bird-eater tarantulas live in burrows on the forest floor. These huge spiders are 11 inches (28 cm) across! When threatened, they rub their leg hairs together to make a hissing noise. They stand on their back legs and throw loose hairs at predators, too.

Goliath Tarantula Dinner

On a separate sheet of paper, unscramble these words to find some more Goliath spider snacks.

1. SGORF
2. EICM
3. ZILRADS

Other spiders catch food using a web. Use your finger to help this spider find the center of its web.

Rain Forests in Danger

We need to protect the rain forests. Large areas are being destroyed. People chop the trees down for wood or clear areas to grow crops and raise farm animals. This puts many species of plants and animals at risk.

Rain forests help our planet. Their trees and plants soak up a harmful gas called carbon dioxide. They produce oxygen, too, which animals and humans breathe.

A quarter of the ingredients in our medicines come from plants in rain forests! Scientists believe there are even more medicines there that we have not discovered yet!

People are clearing the rain forest in Borneo and Sumatra to grow palm oil. Orangutans that live there are in danger of dying out.

These are just some of the hundreds of rain forest animals in danger of dying out. Can you match the names to the pictures? Write your answers on a separate sheet of paper.

- golden tamarin
- orangutan
- jaguar
- tapir

How Can You Help the Rain Forests?

1. Ask your family to buy items that have not harmed the rain forests. Packaging will often say if the product is rain forest-friendly.

2. Have a bake sale to raise money for a rain forest charity.

3. Trees are cut down to make more room for cows. Eating less beef can help stop the rain forest from disappearing.

4. Join a group that protects animals in danger.

Rain Forest Genius Test

Are you a rain forest and jungle genius? Answer these questions to find out.

1 Which layer of the rain forest gets the least sunlight?

a) the canopy

b) the emergent layer

c) the forest floor

2 How can an orange tiger be invisible in a green jungle?

a) They decorate themselves with leaves.

b) The animals they hunt are color-blind.

c) They hide in orange trees.

3 Which of these usually have tails?

a) apes b) monkeys

4 How can you help save the rain forests?

a) Use palm oil from Borneo.

b) Eat more beef.

c) Try to buy items that say they are rain forest-friendly.

5 How do sloths avoid being caught by sharp-eyed predators?

a) They move so slowly their predators don't notice them.

b) They are camouflaged by tiny plants that grow all over their fur.

c) Both a and b.

Answers

Page 5:

B	U	T	T	E	R	F	L	Y	E
E	F	I	N	S	G	B	U	L	N
L	S	G	O	R	I	L	L	A	R
E	V	E	W	T	N	E	T	S	E
P	S	R	T	A	W	U	G	P	S
H	D	V	C	M	G	I	H	R	H
A	C	U	A	N	S	T	N	L	T
N	O	I	A	L	P	N	K	G	O
T	S	R	M	A	C	A	W	I	L
U	O	Q	U	T	V	S	E	R	S

Page 6: A tiger.

Page 9: 1 b, 2 a, 3 c.

Page 11: emergent layer - sugar glider; canopy - sloth; understory - jaguar; forest floor - anteater.

Page 12:

Page 16: The frog might eat the leaf-cutter ant.

Page 17: Raindrop b

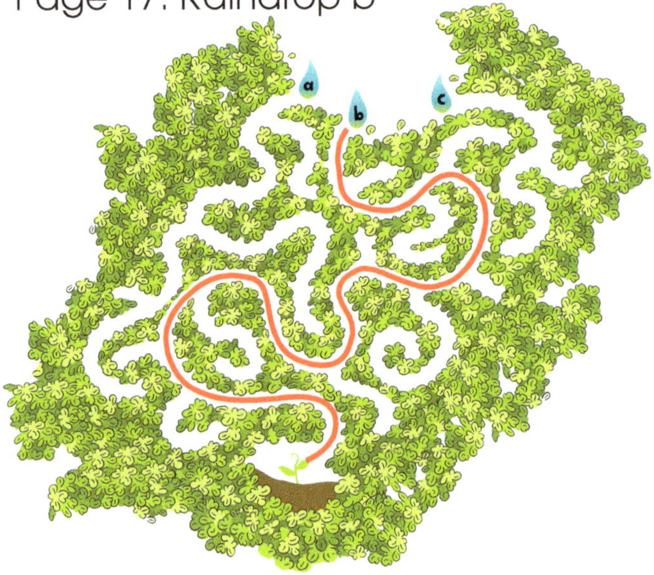

Page 19 top: a = sloth, b = capybara, c = sugar glider, d = poison dart frog

Page 19 bottom:

Page 21: A baby forest elephant.

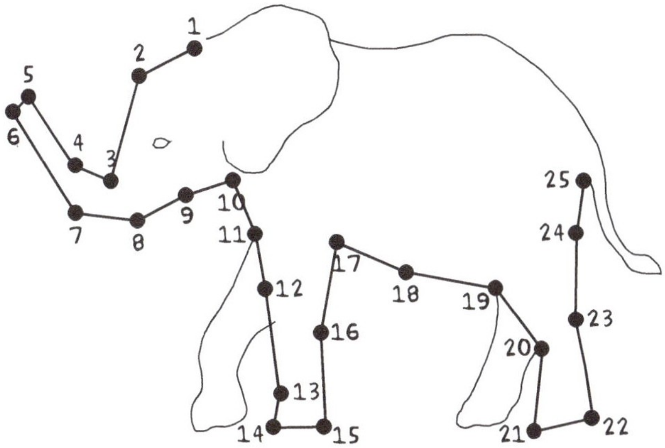

Page 23:

Page 24: A wide beak is good for scooping up lots of candy, but a pointy beak is good for picking candy from between the rocks.

Page 27: Chimpanzees and orangutans are apes. Baboons and golden tamarins are monkeys.

Page 29:

Page 30:

Page 31: Piranhas have very sharp teeth.

Page 32:

Page 33: The cone of modeling clay should be the least wobbly.

Page 30: The frog is bright red and black—the colors of some poison dart frogs.

Page 37: being mainly green and brown helps snakes hide in the green and brown forest.

Page 39 top:

Page 39 bottom:

B	E	F	A	L	M	O	Z	L	D
L	C	A	I	M	A	N	S	E	S
I	A	H	R	S	C	X	E	Y	R
K	P	E	K	T	H	R	E	M	S
W	Y	O	T	N	T	K	I	E	E
O	B	C	R	G	N	I	D	L	L
S	A	S	L	O	T	H	S	R	T
V	R	O	M	L	E	N	K	P	R
B	A	P	I	N	R	S	H	C	U
U	S	S	M	B	I	R	D	S	T

Page 40: a Goliath bird-eater spider

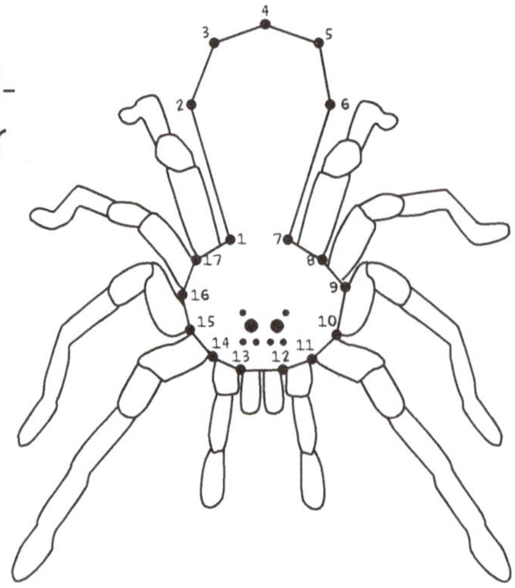

Page 41 top: 1. frogs 2. mice 3. lizards

Page 41 bottom:

Page 43:

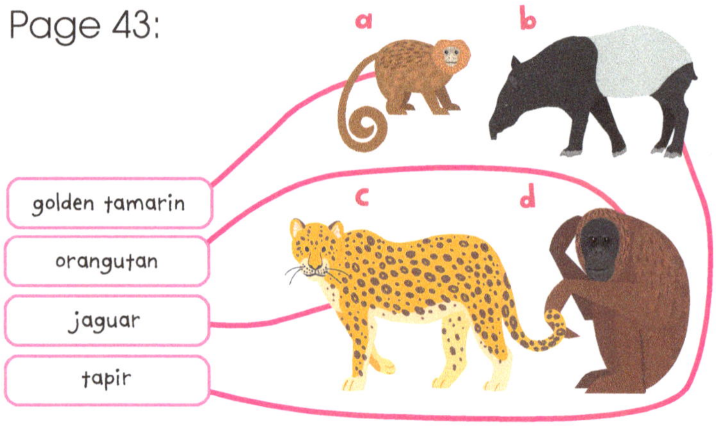

Page 44: 1) c - The forest floor gets the least sunlight. 2) b - The animals they hunt are color-blind. 3) b - monkeys 4) c - Try to buy items that are rain forest-friendly. 5) c - Both a and b.